Sell with NLP

Index

INTRO 4

VENDOR ERRORS 9

TRUST AND NLP 21

CONVERSATIONAL SUGGESTION TECHNIQUES 37

THE VAK MODEL 44

CAPTIVATE THE CUSTOMER 62

ANCHORS IN NLP 70

HYPNOTIC QUESTIONS AND PERSUASIVE SALES 80

THE SWITCH MODE 91

POTENTIATING OR DE-POTENTIATING STATE?
....94

THE RULE OF CONTRAST 104

CLOSE THE SALE 107

CONCLUSIONS..119

DISCLAIMER 121

Intro

When we talk about NLP, that is Neuro-Linguistic Programming, we refer to a communication model and at the same time to a personal development, which starts in the Seventies, where psychotherapy and life coaching are involved and the self-help.

John Grinder and Richard Bandler, founders of this method of interpersonal communication, highlighted how the basis of everything was the identification of a whole series of modalities, aimed at helping everyone to live lives richer in emotions and even more complete.

Why then NLP or following the English acronym NLP (Neuro-Linguistic Program)?
For the simplest of reasons.
Neurological language and processes are closely connected: behavioral patterns have

been learned from experience, and therefore for programming. If you want to achieve certain goals in life, these schemes can also be reorganized.

Neuro-Linguistic Programming is based on multiple facets, both visible in everyday life and the field of sales. And in this book, we will focus on this last aspect, not forgetting anyway examples of the daily routine.

One of the many aspects that distinguish Neuro-Linguistic Programming is that it provides sellers with a series of powerful tools, perfectly able to facilitate the relationship with the customer and, as a logical consequence, to complete the sale.
If you are a seller, you can use these refined NLP tools to update, to integrate and above all to consolidate your skills in this field.

If you think about it, face-to-face sales focus on a myriad of elements, including the creation of a relationship of trust with the customer and persuasive communication. And NLP is a subject that for the past forty years has been explaining just how to communicate in the most efficient way possible. This is why the applications of NLP are closely related to the field of sales.

Everything you say, as a sales professional, how you communicate it to the customer (tone of voice, body posture, facial expression) have a significant impact on both your neurology and that of your interlocutor. This is the ABC of Neuro-Linguistic Programming.

An example can help you better understand the pattern of how the communication mode has a significant impact on who is listening to you: you are a sales manager and one of your collaborators, recently hired by the company, has just made a mistake that led to a failed delivery.

Loss € 1,000.
You look at him, give him a pat on the back and calmly explain his mistake, asserting I AM NOT ANGRY IN YOUR COMPARISONS.

In this case, your collaborator will believe you, because your intonation of the voice and your mimic shows him that as a novice the mistake can be there. Learning is made a mistake, on the other hand. It's not true?

Same situation. Beat your fists on the table where the computers are placed, you tend to gesticulate excessively and you almost shout I AM NOT ANGRY IN YOUR COMPARISONS.
Do you think you are credible in this second case? Even if your words communicate something else, your interlocutor will be anything but convinced.
You did not use a tone of voice typical of a calm person.

Your report does not coincide with the para-verbal communication (as defined in the NLP) Ergo ... let's do two accounts.

With this book, we intend to address all the professionals in the sales and operating in the business world, from door-to-door salespeople to sales managers, from entrepreneurs to managers, but also to all those who have been working on their person for years to have an image better, especially in the workplace. Therefore, the primary aim will be to explain what Neuro-Linguistic Programming is and how to put it into practice to sell better. Step by step you will realize how the tools of NLP are efficient and affordable for everyone.

Vendor errors

What does it mean to sell a product, essentially?
· Close a commercial negotiation which is the essence of the sale
· Pleasure and fascinate the customer which is like saying sell yourself, allowing the interlocutor to appreciate your image (regardless of whether you buy from you or not)
· Can pass on your idea which means that when you conduct a sales negotiation, one of the many intentions of sales agents is to demonstrate the effective goodness of your business proposal

Not always, to use a euphemism, the sales negotiations are concluded with a positive outcome. What affects them sometimes are external factors that have nothing to do with the skill of the seller. The exaggerated price of a product, no matter how good the seller is, will seldom lead the customer to purchase. If that splendid washing machine just put on the market by the Japanese manufacturer on duty has the most sophisticated features but costs maybe 5,000 euros, as much as you may like, those with an income of 1,500 euros a month will hardly buy it. The same applies to an unnecessary good. If the client in question does not need that particular insurance policy, he will not even stop to listen to your proposal. Other times then (potential) customers are really in a hurry and time to devote, they have zero. Therefore, even if you propose a cheaper internet-phone plan than what they currently have, the answer will be negative.

This almost always.

However, sometimes, the seller is wrong (even blatantly) in the way he poses and may not like the potential customer.

A few years ago, the prestigious University of Harvard carried out a study, involving 230 buyers as a sample. What was the result?

12% of the sellers were judged excellent, to 23% an overall positive evaluation was assigned, 38% returned to the average and the beauty of 27% was considered unsuitable for sale. In short, over ¼ of the sellers (not very few) were judged as scarce. This research aims to explain to you that the competition in the sales sector is very high. Only if you are considered excellent or if you are given positive feedback, you are among the sellers who have more or less concrete possibilities to sell. If, on the other hand, you are part of that 38% slice, judged to be average, you are not one of those who make the leap for the business you sell. Ergo, do not expect in terms of salary sea and mountains. The reason is that you cannot differentiate yourself from customers. For the remaining 27%, it is worth studying, learning new approaches, questioning the modus operandi and, if necessary, changing jobs. If the customer is disappointed, annoyed or pissed off, if you are unable to break into his emotional sphere, always try to understand the reason. It is not always the fault of the high price or the economic crisis.

So, here are some reasons that can lead you to a sensational flop in the sale.

YOU ARE'NT CREDIBLE
You can be judged differently, but negatively.

You can look like the seller who aims to sell the item at all costs. It is too nagging and customers prefer to avoid it by turning to another seller. How many times the same product, a seller maybe will sell it and another one doesn't?

If you want to be a skilled salesman, according to one of the fundamental principles of Neuro-Linguistic Programming, you must have the ability to direct the client towards the best choice, according to his needs, giving him all the appropriate advice. Limit yourself to thinking that selling at all costs is the only real and concrete goal is an unforgivable mistake. A satisfied customer will trust you the most and will most likely come back and knock on your door again. A seller confirms to be a seller with a capital V when he has customers who buy from him, but also when the customer is pushed with the utmost naturalness to talk positively about that particular brand, that specific product or that specific service. This causes the most powerful form of advertising possible: word of mouth.

Referring to that research conducted by the University of Harvard, only 18% of sellers fall into this circle. Trust, as you can easily guess, is not reserved for everyone.

YOU CANNOT RELATE YOURSELF WITH CUSTOMERS OF YOUR COMPANY
The approach for each customer is always different. If you are used to interfacing with customers who buy the product regularly and are categorized as inexperienced buyers, the chances of success may be higher than those inherent in higher-level company negotiations. The reason? It is not said that you have the right skills to talk to them. There are many expert customers who, when interviewed, declare that only 1/3 of the sellers has the right skills for negotiations conducted in a workmanlike manner. It is, in fact, urgent to apply more suitable sales techniques.

YOU CANNOT COMMUNICATE IN AN EFFICIENT MANNER FOR ANY REASON THE CUSTOMERS WILL BENEFIT FROM YOUR SALES PROPOSAL
Basically, as a seller, you are called daily to explain what are the real advantages that

the product presents. How can it improve the customer's life? Why is it worth buying? What is better than competing items? This is the ABC of the sale, so much so that over half of the sellers (believe me, it's not a big percentage) can pass this step. At the base of everything, there must be a study of the product that explains simply if it improves the yields, if it reduces the times, if it lowers the costs and if it streamlines the procedures. In short, describing the benefits and advantages to the fullest gives you that extra quid necessary to convince the customer to purchase.

YOU FIND TOO MUCH INDIVIDUALISM
Those who fall into the range of expert buyers often judge sellers too focused on themselves, that is to say on selling at all costs. Often, they lead the negotiation wrongly thinking of how to sell the product as if they were addressing themselves and not the customer they are dealing with. An

excessive focus on one's own needs is a huge mistake, because the customer immediately senses that the seller is not taking care of his interests, but instead only thinks about his agenda and his goals: selling. If the seller is not very interesting in terms of communication, the customer will shrug and go elsewhere. When you sell you always remember to identify the customer's needs first and then focus on your needs.

DO NOT KNOW HOW TO CLOSE THE NEGOTIATION: DO NOT KNOW THE APPROPRIATE CLOSING TECHNIQUES

The sentence, the offer expires today is one of the closing methods with which you can do everything except concluding the sales negotiation. The reason? The customer is too annoyed, as he is with his back against the wall, but this is a boomerang. This is true in life and sales as well. Therefore, never put the customer in the condition of having to decide to take everything immediately or give up. What you need is a softer closing technique to finish the deal. A phrase like this: With an additional investment of just 5,000 euros, you can take advantage of a 4% tax advantage, the possibility of closing the transaction successfully. The reason? The advantage is immediately explained. The customer makes two accounts and if agrees accept.

In this regard, we will devote a chapter on how to effectively close sales negotiations using the powerful tools of Neuro-Linguistic Programming.

SPEAK ABOUT GUARANTEES AND RISKS

With the customer, you must always be transparent and present guarantees and risks in the simplest way possible. When conducting a sales negotiation, you have to present what may not go the right way. If you work in the insurance field, for one thing, this thing is even more obvious. If the deal is described with the most beautiful words in the world, but no signs of guarantees and risks, the customer, especially if he has been burned by previous purchases, could become suspicious and believe that there is something rotten in Denmark. Ergo, he will let it go.

THE ABILITY TO BUILD GOOD INTERPERSONAL COMMUNICATION IS MISSING

Discounted to say that customers feel more confident towards the sellers with which there is human chemistry. The basic interpersonal communication must be good. If therefore, as a seller, you have obvious differences in the communication style with respect to that of the clientele, you behave in an excessively pressing manner, you prove too impatient and do not expect anything other than the customer to put his signature on the contract, look for at all costs to make you the customer's friend ... well, you will end up failing, because you have not been able to weave good interpersonal communication with those on the other side. Making a good impression is essential if you want to be successful in this area.

The feedback, i.e. the final result, is always given by how effective your communication was. If as a seller, you are selling a dishwasher, and explain to the customer that even though it costs like that of a competing brand, it is more powerful and has a better yield in terms of energy and consumption, if you can't sell it, maybe it's because you don't you were able to explain yourself well and, in fact, the interlocutor did not understand you. The advantages of your proposal in commercial terms have not come up. You didn't communicate in the right way to let the customer buy your dishwasher. The feedback you ultimately get is that your method was not perfect for the mindset of the potential buyer. And if this happens for a certain period with many of your customers, it means that your method is wrong and that there is something wrong. They are not incompetent customers. It is not that there is no money around and that there is a crisis. All pretexts. It is your ineffective method. You must change, if necessary, even radically, your modus operandi in the conduct of a sales negotiation. In this respect, you still have a lot to work on your profile. There is always hope. Don't give up!

Summing up, for each of these errors, the tools of NLP can be useful. And you, among the errors, just mentioned, do you recognize someone who frequently commits?

Trust and NLP

As for the origins of NLP, as anticipated, these date back to the 1970s. Everything revolves around the modeling of excellence.

What does it mean? In summary, we study a whole series of subjects, which represent excellence in their field, and we try in every way to understand how they achieve such extraordinary results and performances out of reach of ordinary mortals. Therefore, Neuro-Linguistic Programming is born with the painstaking work of doctors and hypnotherapists. Therefore, it follows that it has nothing scientifically proven.

At the base of the NLP, therefore, there are postulates. Assumptions that are not true at all, but that have a certain utility both in everyday routine and when selling something.

· There is always and, in any case, a positive intention behind most behaviors:

specifically, there is a context within which that particular behavior has a specific value

· When it comes to choosing, the interlocutor always does it for those that are his interests. Or rather, the best choice among the available alternatives is always carried out. This, of course, based on the situation in which he found himself, in relation to the resources possessed. To those who look at it from an external point of view, it often happens that they believe that the decision taken seemed, on the whole, absurd, out of any scheme or worse still totally devoid of any logic. But that is not the point of view of the person concerned who may have antipodal values and beliefs.

· The most skilled communicators, those who know how to fascinate and entertain those who listen to them, put into practice any act of communication, be it verbal, para-verbal or non-verbal, and behavior. If you are a professional in the field of sales, have you already conducted a difficult negotiation which in the end was not successful? Once the negotiation is over, maybe you will happen to say VA BENE, DAI. IN THE BEGINNING, THIS CUSTOMER WAS REALLY IMPOSSIBLE.

In reality, based on this postulate of NLP, it is not the client that is impossible, but, on the contrary, you, the seller, have not understood what positive intentions harbored in your personality at that particular moment. So, giving you a sharp refusal, returning to the previous postulate, he did nothing but take what for him, in that specific time frame, was the best possible decision between the two options available, YES / NO.

· Living without communicating is not possible. Even if you keep silent, always communicate something. It is your body, through posture, that always transmits something. The interlocutor always interprets every single gesture you make in a precise way. Even the words you say, if they are misunderstood, have a significant relevance on the progress of a speech or at the final outcome of a sales negotiation. Therefore, remember: even when you are still and shut up, communicate something.

· The map is not the territory. What does it mean? Synthetically, what we see as reality is not the absolute reality. Each of us has filters with which we perceive the mode differently. We will go deeper into the aforementioned topic in the next chapters, giving a concrete example of you and two friends going to the cinema to watch a film and, despite having seen the same show, you have focused on different aspects. Distortions, generalizations, and removals are obvious aspects of the information acquisition process. Objective reality is a rare exception. Even if two or more people live the same experience, even at the same time, after some time, they will remember it in a very different way, because they have filtered the distinctive traits in a different way. Another example: try asking an engaged couple to describe the day of their first date. Well, there is no doubt that the situation is the same. Nevertheless, they will not describe it in the same way, since the sensations are always different, because their filters on reality do not coincide. What escaped him is firmly in her mind. What remains impressed in the map of the two are not the same memories. Each of us is unique and distant from others in terms of identity, values , and beliefs.

The Neuro-Linguistic Programming in the field of sales proves useful for a whole series of heterogeneous reasons. Let's quickly review them:

· Create long-term and successful relationships with various customers
· Prevent the customer from objecting during the negotiation

- Prevent the customer from being skeptical or reticent during the negotiation
- Identify in an immediate manner which are the decisional strategies that ensure that the customer is positively directed to the purchase or that the contract is closed with his signature
- Communicate in the best possible way, paying the utmost attention to the words adopted, to the tone of the voice with which you address the customer and before to your body language (which always communicates something)
- Make your emotional state the best possible ally

You are a chief of staff and you have to evaluate two salesmen: the first sells 45 products to 50 customers, while the second sells only 7. Which one will you choose? Almost certainly the first one, as he proved to be more skilled. More persuasive. In short, excellence in the field of sales.

If you want to sell more or better, the number one rule that underlies Neuro-Linguistic Programming is that you have to make sure that customers are comfortable with you. This means that in most cases, customers tend to express positive feedback to you when you can give them your pleasant company. If customers are comfortable with you, they will come back to you. They will look for you, because you will be considered a special seller, able not only to sell products and services, but also to give moments of carefree, relaxing situations and positive energy.

Charisma with customers is essential to conclude a sales negotiation. As a salesperson, can you increase this dowry? Trust is the basic element. An excellent interpersonal relationship between the seller and the buyer is precisely about trust. Being cordial, cheerful, trustworthy also serves to convey confidence. If a customer speaks well of you to other potential customers, they will turn to you for the logic of word of mouth. If the customer is suspicious or suspicious of you, you will be unlikely to be able to conclude a contract. Is it not so?

The trust process is in fact confirmed as the essential step of the entire persuasive process, crucial for the customer to be encouraged to buy. Although trust should be built gradually when selling, there are many professionals in the commercial field who ignore this golden rule and tend to underestimate it, immediately presenting the product/service. Acting in this way is a gamble, given that the positive outcome of the negotiation between the parties is already in jeopardy. And this even before the sales negotiation started. Before the operations begin, you must have the talent to convey the above feeling to the customers you interface with: I FIND THIS PLEASANT SELLER. IT IS LIKE YOU KNOW IT FROM A LIFE.

Simple to say, but how do you create trust?

The tracing process, also known as mirroring or mirroring, turns out to be decisive in this perspective, as well as being one of the most useful NLP tools. This is the assumption of the posture of your interlocutor. In an empathic and trusting relationship, the interlocutors, even the seller, and the buyer tend to have the same posture. How is mirroring created? When we talk about tracing, the most explicit reference has directly to do with customer mirroring. The implementation of this mirroring can be verbal, para-verbal, non-verbal and extra-verbal, also known as emotional.

Eye, always to the NOT SAID, because it communicates over 70% of what are the real intentions of the customers with whom you interact in everyday life, regardless of what they are then telling you at that precise moment.

ARE YOU INTENDED TO BUY MY PRODUCT? A yes, unconvinced in body posture and anything but energetic, is a yes only in verbal communication, but not in para-verbal communication. Translated in simple terms, at the time of signing the contract or buying, with each it will probably result in a refusal. I DO NOT KNOW. I HAVE TO THINK. CURRENCY AND SEE. I WILL LET YOU KNOW. These are the most common maxims among skeptical customers.

In short, a YES pulled with nails and teeth, and a convinced SI, everything is except the same thing. They have two different weights.
For example, a wine seller engages in negotiations with a customer.

After 5 minutes they find a common anchor and begin to talk about how nice it is to sip a good glass of Hausmannhof Pinot Noir Haderburg. The two drink it together, they start talking and the moment they talk about a topic that both of them care about, the client will imitate the seller's posture. The unconscious of the seller will agree with that of the buyer because he will be strongly intent on learning more about that particular topic. That is why, when the seller has a posture with his chin resting on his fist, intent on listening to what the buyer has to say, the buyer will also tend to bring his chin to his fist. If after some time the customer speaks with his arms folded, when it is up to the seller to do so, it is very likely that traveling on the same wavelength as the interlocutor, even after a while he will tend to talk, having arms folded. Never do it immediately, otherwise, the customer will begin to suspect that you are imitating his position on purpose.

We need to know how to do it with a certain nonchalance.

Mirroring your client's posture is a kind of non-verbal ballet that drives you to be more likely to like it. The client's unconscious will receive the message that you are similar to him as the main information. If the customer opens up more and more towards you, it means that he has empathized with you. You hooked him, but at the same time, he hooked you.

Not only do you trace the customer, but it is the customer that follows you.
This mirroring must be natural, otherwise, it is a manipulation. And if the customer senses that you are imitating him just to please him, well ... don't be disappointed if the sales negotiation ends. Breaking the ice, you end up softening the initial impact and you'll find yourself in the condition of having to score a goal in an empty net. Selling the product or signing the contract will certainly be easier.

There is no more efficient way to be tuned to the same wavelength as your customers. Demonstrating that you are like your client will necessarily mean being like him and then the latter will trust you more. Result? The customer will want to buy from you! Tracing behavioral nuances is not easy. However, asking the right questions to the current client will allow you to gain his trust. Finding commonalities is also the first step in undertaking any kind of business relationship. Upstream there must be careful work by the seller that leads the customer to conclude BETWEEN YOU AND ME, THAT WE REALLY HAVE VERY MUCH IN COMMON. Tracing is the most successful method for synchronizing seller and buyer. The reason? Synchrony is synonymous with the union of intents. And in the sale, you are in tune with your client or not. And to greater harmony, higher percentages will inevitably correspond to conclude the sales negotiation in a positive manner with the maximum satisfaction of both parties.

Being calm and smiling from the first contact with the customer, being calm, starting communication with shared themes both by you and by him will allow you to start on the right foot.

A customer enters a clothing store after looking at the window. If the seller uses the phrase: I HAVE NOTIFIED THAT HE WAS LOOKING CAREFULLY ON THAT WHITE SHIRT! It will increase the likelihood of purchase by the customer. All this because with a simple and concise beginning sentence that comes directly to the heart of the matter, the seller has proved himself able to create harmony with his counterpart, having immediately understood his emotions and his needs. Knowing how to train this innate talent is very useful to succeed in the world of business negotiations. And NLP with its multiple instruments plays a crucial role in

this sense. Train with your friends, your family, your partner or your collaborators.
In the long run, you will feel more confident around your personality, you will be more inclined to dialogue and you will be more inclined to listen.
Seeing is believing!

Summing up, trust, harmony, and empathy are values that must be created right from the start in every type of dialogue. I enjoy it or not, first impressions count!
Then clearly as a skilled salesman, you will need to be able to make these values last as long as possible. And in the entire sales negotiation and in its conclusion. If you notice on the way that the relationship with your client is starting to fail, because you are not trusting, being in harmony and empathizing, well ... you have to have the talent to find these qualities, otherwise you run the serious risk of creating distance with the counterparty.

As you can easily guess, the percentages of finalizing the sale will tend to drop dramatically. And this must not happen for anything in the world. You must always be able to feel close to your interlocutor, you must try to be as equal as possible to your profile, you must intercept his needs, you must also support him and only after all this you can propose your ideas to solve any problems.

This is the basic idea of Neuro-Linguistic Programming applied to sales. Your proposal is aimed at improving the customer's lifestyle. By offering positive emotions to buyers, they will have the pleasure of buying from you. And they will come back to visit you again. Enhance your communication, adapt your attitude to that of the customer and don't just stare at your product.

Conversational suggestion techniques

If your declared goal is to become the number one in the field of sales, one of the basic values of your professional creed must be to love the interpersonal relationships that you can weave with your customers. As we have already said in the previous chapter, the relationship of trust must be built immediately, to arouse interest and obtain the highest esteem from the client.

On the basis of what the principles of NLP indicate, the salesman who learns to resort to forms and techniques of conversational suggestion manages to create indelible emotions in the mind of the interlocutor and to have the road paved towards the closing of the sale. All in an ethical and efficient way.

Along the same lines as athletes and champions in the world of sports, who use autosuggestion to improve their performance, as a skilled salesman, you can bet everything on these techniques. In the long run, you will see how customers will be more receptive to what you communicate in sales negotiations because you could increase their sensitivity about what you say.

How to communicate attractively to the customer?

Assuming that there are many approaches, Neuro-Linguistic Programming indicates four techniques of conversational suggestion that are worthy of attention. Here they are one by one in detail.

Verbal suggestions: in the role of the seller, verbal suggestions allow you to create expectations. The words prove to be extremely practical tools for sending suggestions to the customer. How many times have you read the phrase in the description of the latest generation smartphone camera: WILL YOU REMEMBER FROM THE PERFORMANCE OF THE NEW IPHONE CAMERA? The seller assumes that the customer is interested in the fact that the customer is interested in what the camera of the new iPhone allows him to do and that his message is in effect a prophecy that is realized. Understanding the psychology of verbal suggestion is crucial to achieving excellent results when you sell. The main motivation lies in the fact that the latter is characterized by the ability to influence, in a more or less decisive way, the pattern of thinking of customers. Whether these are actual or potential.

Non-verbal suggestions: gestures and facial expressions always communicate content. The skilled and experienced salesman can perfectly interpret what is not said with traditional communication. Let's start from the assumption that gestures, even those that are more insignificant, add emphasis to communication, as well as a more or less evident persuasive impact. If when you sell, your body language follows that of the interlocutor, you will have more chances of being successful, because even if you are unconsciously telling them LOOK (or better LISTEN), I AM AS YOU! The smile, just as an example, helps (and a lot) to ensure that the client lowers the barriers of his subconscious and that a highway opens up towards the conclusion of the negotiation. There is no better way than to create a relaxing environment with a beautiful smile. Intra-verbal suggestions: fundamental because of a highly persuasive communication. How to get them? Through intonation. Knowing how to give words the greatest possible effectiveness and the ability to transform them into action commands are qualities that only very few vendors can leverage. A phrase like

IMAGINE HOW MUCH HAPPY WIFE WILL BE IN THE MOMENT YOU PUT IT ON THE NECK THIS SPLENDID COLLIER will immediately give the customer a state of well-being, precisely because the adjective HAPPY will help create this pleasant feeling of happiness, precisely. And you, do you know how to produce persuasive messages? Can you pronounce them with the right pitch of the voice? If so, you're certainly on the right track to becoming an ace in the sales world.

Extra-verbal suggestions: when words, facial expressions, gestures and intonation of the voice are in a perfect and absolute state of synergy, an emotional process is triggered which is highly persuasive. The skilled salesman, not surprisingly, is the one who has the talent to speak between the lines. The listener thinks in every respect to be the source of that particular idea. A simple example of extra-verbal suggestion is the following. If you tell a friend, WE GO

TO THE BAR TO GET A BEER, you're giving him a command. Saying instead the sentence DOES A LITTLE HOT TONNING. DON'T YOU YEAR TO BE ONLY CLOSED AT HOME? Beer? it's all another story. The reason? The friend is persuaded to go down with us to the city, because the message is conveyed that loneliness on a hot evening is unlucky and that the heat is fought with a nice cold beer, in friendship. The beauty? Your friend was probably already aware that being alone at home in the summer was sad in itself, but you communicated to your sub-conscious with your message. Imagine how powerful an extra verbal suggestion in the field of sales can be. DON'T YOU HAVE A BORN TO GET YOU LOAN THE SMARTPHONE TO MAKE PHOTOS? it is for example a way in which the person who sells can convince those who really do not want to feel right to switch to a new device. The effects of this communication are invisible but only in an apparent way. Because with a conversational tone the person concerned is confronted with a problem on which it may be appropriate to take the necessary countermeasures.

In principle, if you want to become a protagonist in the world of sales, train by following these four conversational suggestion techniques even in everyday life. After a while, you will find out how you have become persuasive!

The VAK Model

Human beings perceive reality through the five senses: sight, hearing, smell, taste, and touch. These are not other filters through which reality is sieved and based on those your preferences are, you tend to focus on one sense rather than another. Here is an example that can prove really useful to the already mentioned postulate of NLP, according to which the map is not the territory.

You go with two friends to the cinema to see a film that is talked about so much. While watching, you may be more attracted by special effects, because you are a visual type, your friend maybe more from music and soundtracks, because he is a more auditory type, while your other friend, maybe more from emotions that the cinematographic show gave him because it is a more kinesthetic type.

Once you get out of the movie theater, you and your two friends are sure to watch the same movie. Nevertheless, you will tell it differently. The reason? At the base, you have focused on different aspects that you and others may not have noticed. If, for example, from a visual point of view, you have focused on special effects, it is not said that you will have taken into consideration the fact that that given soundtrack had already been used in a successful 1988 movie. We tend to have a preference for a sense rather than to another. Neuro-Linguistic Programming has certainly not invented the five senses but has integrated them into a new model. However, this discipline shows that there are people more stimulated by the visual system, others more by the auditory system, others even more by the kinesthetic system. We speak of the VAK model, where the V indicates visual, the A auditory, the K stands for kinesthetic. In brackets O.G., where O stands for olfactory and G for gustatory.

The visual channel is the sensorially preferential channel for most of the interlocutors when it comes to receiving information. Visual types see things. They must, therefore, see the items you sell. The auditory types, on the other hand, must feel things. You have to tell him things. The classic consumers who blindly trust word of mouth, who maybe buy on friends' advice or because their neighbor told them. Finally, the kinesthetic types need to try the products on themselves, the reference article must always and in any case confer a situation of pleasantness or well-being.

In reference to the purchase of a blue velvet jacket, the visual type puts it on and looks in the mirror, because it wants to see how it looks. The auditory one perhaps acquires it because his work colleague tells him that as a garment, he is very practical. Finally, the kinesthetic one wears it and finds out if he is at ease. And yet, it's the same blue velvet jacket.

Yet another example. That of the car. When buying, the kinesthetic wants to sit inside. Almost driving it, to see if it feels comfortable in the cockpit. He wants to smell the scent of the interior. The visual one wants to see more models and judge what suits them best. Finally, the auditory one will collect the opinions and listen to the comments of those who have this car.

The beauty of this speech is that of visual, auditory, kinesthetic, olfactory and gustatory types, there are none. I miss the shadow. Rather, it is fair to say that there are several representational strategies of reality. This means that the five senses are all active within us, but these are put in a different sequence. From your own you have the access channel that ensures you can interface with the outside world: you seller, use this channel immediately when you meet the customer for the first time. Its use is not assiduous. Then there is your processing channel it allows you to better process information, to reflect, to reason and to make decisions. Whether they are right or wrong. It follows that as a seller, you are required to use the aforementioned channel on an ongoing basis. Perhaps it is the most widely used one.

It is no coincidence that many scholars of Neuro-Linguistic Programming tools applied to sales also define it as a preferential channel, as well as a channel of influence, as it is useful to persuade and to convince customers to buy. Then there is the deep channel, also referred to as the inner channel, whose basic mission is all centered around the personal sphere that is as intimate as ever. You tend to use it not by chance only and exclusively with the customers with whom you are in confidence. It is rarely used with few individuals.

As we mentioned earlier, these channels are sequenced. What does it mean? That in essence there is the access channel, then the processing channel immediately after and finally the inner one. By combining the three channels, visual, auditory and kinesthetic, a maximum of six representational systems of reality will be eliminated:

1. VAK (Visual, Auditory, Kinesthetic)
2. VKA (Visual, Kinesthetic, Auditory)
3. AVK (Auditory, Visual, Kinesthetic)
4. AKV (Auditory, Kinesthetic, and Visual)
5. KAV (Kinesthetic, Auditory and Visual)
6. KVA (Kinesthetic, Visual and Auditory)

Having the visual in access, the auditory in elaboration and the kinesthetic in the inner one means that to start a successful communication the first terms must be connected to the visual sphere, then resort to verbs pertaining to the auditory area to create empathy in regarding your own way of deciding, and finally adopting idioms related to the emotional sphere. In this case, the matching will be confirmed even more solid.

To the buyer who perhaps prefers the use of the visual sphere, to say in the role of the seller phrases such as LOOKING WITH INTEREST IN HIS PERSPECTIVE or I SEE CLEARLY THAT WHICH APPEARS TO BE HIS POINT OF VIEW, I WOULD LIKE TO TAKE A LOOK AT THIS PRODUCT or even HOW DO YOU SEE THE SITUATION? it means to have perfectly understood how its channels are put in sequence. In this case, it is wise to always use expressions related to the world of images.

The situation with those with a tendentially auditory pattern is different. This is the world of sounds. So, expressions such as WHAT YOU LIKE PLEASE FEEL HARMONY WITH YOUR POSITION, I HAVE NOT COME HERE ONLY TO FEEL MEANING HOW MUCH COSTS THIS ARTICLE OR THEN I FEEL IN FULL TUNING WITH WHAT I HAVE JUST LISTENED

TO, WHAT I HAVE STILL FEEL MORE BELLS will allow you to fascinate customers who filter reality in the first place, focusing on sounds and noises.

If, on the other hand, customers have particularly sophisticated kinesthetic patterns, ways of saying how they MUST NEVER FEEL UNDER EXAMINATION, I HAVE BUTTERFLIES IN THE BELLY, CAN I TOUCH IT? (ed in reference to an object just seen in the window) or HAS A HOT TEMPERAMENT, CAN I SIT ABOVE? or it still HAS A SOLAR CHARACTER will certainly strike their attention.

What I intend to convey to you, in this case, is that by using the right verbs when you sell an article, you have a better chance of catching up with customers. We often use verbal predicates, expressions, and idioms in the most random way possible. However, don't underestimate it. An efficient strategy based on the right use of representational systems gives you the advantageous possibility of making inroads into the hearts of the interlocutors and buyers. But beware that it is not that your interlocutors use only one channel exclusively. The cataloging of the consumer limited to a single channel would be a generalization, given that each individual use both the visual and the auditory channel, as well as the kinesthetic channel. Your seller skill, according to the principles of NLP, consists in identifying also how the representational systems of those who have every interest in buying are disposed, turning to your professionalism. We, therefore, use all three representational channels. However, there is always one that we prefer over others.

In the course of a mediation, sales-oriented or not, the principles of PNL indicate that the speaker, when he uses the preferential channels of the interlocutor, has more chances to fascinate him. There is the talk of calibration, understood as a talent or skill in understanding the listener's mood and, above all, noting what turns out to be his state changes. Therefore, calibration is essential to create a harmonious relationship between people. Paying attention to the main aspects of whoever is in front of you, starting from the physical presence and then continuing with the intonation of the voice, the expressions of the face, the movements of the hands and so on, is fundamental to understand if the one you are talking to, at the moment he is about to change his mood. For example, you're talking to an angry friend, because he was disappointed. You console him, saying that it can happen. You give him the classic pat on the back and smile. Within a few moments, his body posture, his tone of voice, his facial expression will be different than at the moment. By studying people, starting with breathing and eye movement, you can really sense a myriad of things.

It is about calibration if the rapport is established. What is it? Precisely a process by which we first establish and then, over time, make a good relationship between people more solid, where trust between the parties is the essential element. If the listener trusts you (and your words) you have already earned good points. The reason? There is harmony between the parties. On this point a clarification is crucial: the rapport is not eternal. What do you mean? Once established a rapport, overall good with the interlocutor on duty who can also be a customer, well ... this does not last to infinity. If you see your childhood friends as a one-off, you will have the opportunity to establish the rapport for every child you see them. Since knowledge is already good overall, we find that we lose less time because we do not need to start from scratch. To sum up, establishing rapport means defining the primary representational system, through active and participatory listening.

In the perspective of rapport, pacing certainly plays an essential role: it is a process whose basic mission is to access the model of the interlocutor's world. Therefore, always of the customer, when explicit reference is made to the GNP oriented to the commercial area. If a buyer speaks quietly, slowly, articulating the answers well and finds himself facing a seller who is too sure of himself, annoyingly loud, pacing is not set on common sense criteria. The same goes for the waiter who gives her to a customer who has just entered the restaurant and hears you speak. WHAT DO I TAKE THEM TO THE TABLE? THEREFORE, YOU LOVE ME ... how many times have you witnessed a scene like this in person? It may seem insignificant, but believe me, it is not at all.

Respecting the global vision of the interlocutor is very important.

Not doing it in a sales deal is really an unforgivable mistake, because you are playing the chance of ending it positively. In the first case, the customer spoke in a low voice because maybe he wanted privacy. The seller did not consider this aspect, not caring and even being heard by third parties. In the second case, the waiter has formally treated the customer (as it should be), while the latter is not. Acting in these ways, the result will have as a common denominator the fact that you will NEVER SELL, also because you will embarrass the person you are talking to.

How can you notice if you were actually able to create rapport with the customer?

The calibration allows you to observe the interlocutor and to perceive his reactions in every single phase of the pacing process. If after a short time, the person you are communicating with shows you signs of trust, it means that you have worked really well upstream. If he smiles when you talk to him, if he looks at you interested, if he asks and informs himself, because maybe he intends to go into the technical features of the article you are proposing, it means that everything goes smoothly like oil. Conversely, if when you talk to him, the potential buyer keeps his distance, he is not enthusiastic, well, these are negative signs. Urge a turn to complete the trade negotiation.

Furthermore, if the relationship between you seller and the customer is established, the latter will consider you a real guide: you are the one who will lead him in a new direction, that is to say towards the road that leads the buyer to purchase the product. You guide the interlocutor towards your goal: SELL! I'll sell you this white cashmere sweater, because it's soft, with a high neck, warm against the cold winter cold, always fashionable and perfect for every look, from the most elegant to the sportiest. And the customer will think about doing it, because he trusts you, follows you, appreciates the transparency of your business proposal and has been able to present him with that object. Even if he didn't need it at the beginning. But you, who know how to sell everything, have brought out a need for it.

Returning to the VAK discourse, clearly, you too are using a strategy of representational systems. In principle, that of expression coincides with the access channel (for the note the first channel).

You communicate with the first channel, but what stimulates you beyond measure is the second channel.

Processing. And the experience of a salesman comes out when he manages to identify more or less immediately what his second channel is. After doing a bit of tracing on the first channel, it is better to increase the mirroring workloads on the second channel. In this way, the empathy you will create with the client will be higher than the average. And widely, as well.

It is only the second channel that allows you to approach the person who is with you the best, making him stay in a state of well-being and making the company enjoyable.

But now the $ 1 million question. How can the careful seller decode what is the customer's access channel, what is the buyer's processing system and what is the consumer's intimate scheme?

The Neuro-Linguistic Programming provides the seller with a varied list of highly refined instruments. The tone of voice, cadence, rhythm and eye movements are among these.

Before doing so on customers, try asking your friends the following question: HOW WAS YOUR DAY? If you think about it, looking up to the right or the left, it will make a lot of reference to the visual sphere. If before answering, you look sideways, in a horizontal position, to the right or the left, it makes a lot of reference to the auditory sphere. Finally, if before thinking, he thinks looking down, to the right or the left, well...then we are dealing with a tendentially kinesthetic type.

To conclude, always keep in mind the type of question you ask the actual or potential customer.

It is obvious that if you discuss with him on your favorite dish, most often the interlocutor, before answering will look down to the right or left, because the kinesthetic component is the one that is most involved.

Ditto if you ask him which is the film you love the most, it is normal that he will tend to look upwards, given that the visual component is the one pulled the most. Finally, if you ask him what your musical piece of the heart is, it is common that his gaze will be directed to the right or left side horizontally since the auditory side is the one that ends up prevailing. Only in the face of neutral questions, will come out what will be the representational system on which the customer relies more. Talking about the pluses and minuses right away with the customer allows you to understand the thing right away and to use the right verbal predicates and the appropriate sayings to anchor it to your business proposal.

If you are careful about how they are exposed, customers, even if implicitly, end up revealing whether they are visual, aural or kinesthetic types.

Captivate the customer

On how you might be able to fascinate your interlocutor, whether he is a customer or a recipient of your messages, rivers of ink have indeed been written. Of magic formulas, so to speak, there are indeed plenty of them. There are several techniques to get the attention of the customer listening to you. This is little but sure. However, to become good communicators, you always need to understand who you have in front of you.

The logic of win-win, that is to say, I win-you win, is certainly much appreciated, because no one is unhappy and discontent is a feeling that has no roots. In a negotiation, as a seller, you certainly come out as a winner, but even the customer who listens to you confirms to be a counterpart who comes out victorious because he travels in full harmony with your business proposal. You complete the transaction and win; the buyer gets something in return (which can be a benefit) and wins too.

Being empathetic is an added value for everyone who sells something. What does this adjective mean? To have a common foothold in the client, to share his schemes, his vision of the world focused on beliefs and values.

A seller who has a blue tie who finds himself in front of a customer wearing only blue ties has a much better chance of concluding a transaction positively than a seller who does not wear a tie and in the eyes of that particular customer loses reliability, because maybe consider the jacket and tie look essential in the business world. This is just an example of how even the smallest of things, apparently irrelevant, can actually affect the performance of a given mediation.

Be careful though. If you are selling and you realize that your beliefs are in disagreement with those of the client, you must bring the question WORTH THE PENALTY ENTERING EMPATHY WITH THIS CERTAIN CUSTOMER? The answer will always be subjective. For example, if you sell but you have a sporting style and you are obliged to interact with high company customers, well, willingly or not, if you want to be successful in this world, you will have to distort your look. There is no way to keep it. Of Steve Jobs selling iPhones and iPads with black sweaters, jeans and sneakers, there are very few.

This is even more evident when personal opinions come into play in commercial negotiations. In order to avoid going against the customer, increasing the distance from what is his point of view, well...it is worth changing the subject. If necessary, also with an excuse.

Why is empathy a fundamental value, to be honest not only in the context of Neuro-Linguistic Programming but also in the daily routine? Being open to others gives you the considerable advantage of having more chances to be persuasive and to expand the map of the personal world. Result? You will change for the better. This does not mean that you are going to distort your being, but simply that you will have a more complete view of the real needs of the customers with whom you interface every day. This is an adaptation and flexibility in perceiving that there are changes taking place in the outside world, that of the business and that to be successful in the sales branch, it is urgent to make changes in your style. The beauty is that you're going to expand what's inside you.

We have already spoken of it in the previous chapters of the tracing method, also known as mirroring. We have in fact seen that creating empathy with the customer allows you to tune in to a very deep level, managing to assess their needs and needs more subtly. The thing is not trivial, because it allows you to differentiate yourself from other professionals in the sale, because you have been almost (I almost repeat) to create a sort of telepathy with who you are interacting.

There is however a rapport generator that is worth investigating. The rapport on values and beliefs. Both are fundamental pillars of our existence. Knowing what the values and beliefs of your customers are, i.e. their motivational fuel, is very useful when you approach them. It is fundamentally useful, especially for negotiation, to respect them, as they constitute the nerve center of your person.

You are selling a natural supplement and the customer declares you to be vegan. You are not a seller. It will be a wise choice, although you have a different view of the world, do not get into the heart of the subject.

To respond to one of his statements, saying I BELIEVE THAT THE VEGAN STYLE IS WRONG is a huge mistake in the negotiation because it means to tear up his vision of the world.

You're literally snatching the pages of his values and beliefs. Never brutally attack the values and beliefs of those in front of you. Even more in the business branch. At best, the customer will not find your company pleasant and will drop you immediately. In these cases, it is good that you do not express yourself. Shut up. Silence is golden. You are not expressing your opinion to the customer. The latter will not feel attached to the values and you, as a prudent salesman, will not have created any distance to you. You are neither distorted nor expressed false judgments. Share only what you feel like sharing and don't expose yourself to what you disagree with. Even in the most absolute manner. By leaning against his positions, you will make mismatching and you will affect your relationship with him. As a good communicator, in the sales sector, you are always 100% responsible for both the results obtained and the missed goals.

Respecting the values and beliefs of the client, most naturally and spontaneously possible, will certainly make you feel positive. Creating a relationship of this kind helps to create a solid and lasting bond with those who want to buy from you. Doing it artificially, in a deliberate and not unconscious way, because maybe you have guessed a couple of values and beliefs of the one who is in front of you, well...it will rarely lead you to the intention you want. Never be hypocrites. Even more in the commercial sector. It's a boomerang.

A seller of children's items initially finds empathy with the client. Then, entering into the heart of the negotiation, it turns out that the woman strongly believes in the principles of the family.

The seller, who may not have this belief, tells her BEH, EVEN FOR ME THE FAMILY COMES BEFORE EVERYTHING, it can be good once, twice, customers can open up with him.

However, if it is discovered, it will be considered hypocritical and the sale will not go through. Willing or not, even the most skilled of sellers always end up returning to their own world map and it will come out that they have no interest in the family.

Sharing values and beliefs to be successful must always take place in a sincere, honest, spontaneous, natural and open manner. Only in this way, the synergy between the parts will be strong and will have solid roots.

The more you integrate your world map with the values and beliefs you like, the more you will be open to a character. To create empathy with the person in charge, always being attentive to what he says, decode his world map and understand what his real beliefs are. All this will eventually help you in the world of communication.

Anchors in NLP

How many times listening to a particular song, sniffing a specific perfume, do you immediately think of a precise state of mind, perhaps a pleasant moment in the past? There are many external factors that allow you to recall an internal state. These are precisely the anchors. From a stimulus coming from the external environment, you are able to relive a specific situation experienced in the first person. Be it pleasant or not.

Thus, an anchor offers you the opportunity to jump back into your mind, to access a potential state of your experience, to anchor it, that is to say, to fix it in your mind through a gesture, through a word, through smell, and finally take it with you. In this way, you will have been able to create a neuro-emotional switch that you can always reuse, especially when you feel it seriously. Do you have any idea how many times a pleasant memory of the past drives out a negative moment?

The first to speak of conditioning was Ivan Pavlov, an established Russian ethologist, and physiologist, who lived at the turn of the nineteenth and twentieth centuries. His studies on the conditioned reflex announced in 1903 earned him the Nobel Prize for Medicine and Physiology the following year. His most famous experiment is known as Pavlov's dog test. Before feeding the animal, Pavlov preceded the sound of a bell. In this first phase, no salivary secretion is detected. Subsequently, Pavlov supplied the meat to the dog and the stimulus was activated. The next phase of the test consisted of making the dog ring the bell, before giving him food. To conclude, in the third and final phase of the experiment, the sound of the bell corresponded to a salivary stimulus of the dog, despite not being given the meat. In short, at the sound of the bell, the dog already had the mouth-watering, because he expected to eat. It is, therefore, the sound of the bell that became in effect the conditioned reflex. The end result of Pavlov's test is that the brain is able to control physiological behaviors and not just social ones.

On a physiological level, a synapse had been created between an external stimulus and an internal state of mind. What does this talk have to do with the field of Neuro-Linguistic Programming combined with sales? First of all, let's say that in order for an anchor between an internal state of mind and an externally conditioned reflex to take effect, the timing varies from three weeks to one month. This is also known as adaptive behavior to new habits. A new habit is created substantially in this time frame.

So, if for a period of time between twenty-one and thirty days, you have a certain behavior or use a new object or associate an external stimulus to an internal state, an anchor is created.

However, the anchor can also be created in more immediate times. But in this case, the emotions must be really strong. The Maori dance, the famous Haka, performed by the All Blacks, the very strong and dreaded New Zealand national rugby team is rightly among the most popular anchorages of all. That dance, at the moment it is made, aims to arouse awe in the adversaries and to recall on the rugby field, the same energy that the ancestors of the Maoris had before going to war.

A concrete test can be useful to describe to you at best which role the anchors play in the field of GNP combined with sales.

Identify a negative feeling, something for which you may still have a strong regret. Try to hold it firmly in your hand. Combine this with the first color that comes to mind, the first shape that comes to mind and something you can associate, be it a sound or a taste. In general, for these situations, many are those who combine dark colors, black, gray, brown or purple, unpleasant sensations, tastes like bitter, sour or sour and unpleasant sounds like a loud noise, a buzz or a whistle.

Then get up, relax, move your body (arms, shoulders, legs) with the intention of breaking a pattern. Switch to thinking about a pleasant situation. What stimulus do you associate with this? What color comes to mind? Do you associate smells or sounds with this? In these cases, bright or relaxing colors (red, yellow, green or blue) prevail, melodious sounds, intense aromas. Get up, relax again, move your body again, always to break the pattern and finally think back to the bad feeling or your regret. Then try to think of the positive memory. Pause and ask yourself the question: THE POSITIVE REMEMBER WAS ABLE TO BREATHE THE NEGATIVE ONE? In many cases, the answer is yes. What does it mean? This anchor was able to improve your mood.

Or again. Music is also fundamental to sell a product when the client, in turn, associates a soundtrack that reminds him of something relevant. In 1985 Rocky IV was released. Numerous gyms put the soundtrack of when Rocky Balboa began training in the farmhouse ad hoc: music training Vage DiCola or Hearts on Fire by John Cafferty & The Beaver Brown Band. Result? He trained with greater intensity. Isn't this an artificially created anchor?

Going back to the business world, the skilled salesman is the one who manages to bring back to the customer a pleasant memory through an anchorage. A concrete example of anchoring in the field of sales is the following. A seller of insurance policies (a product that is certainly not the most exciting to sell) enters a fishmonger. Objective, sell your policy to the retailer. After the classic pleasantries, on the questions inherent to his business, the astute salesman who has already looked far and wide at the store, refers to a photograph, where a guy who has a big tuna in his hands is immortalized. WHILE I WAS WAITING TO SPEAK TO YOU, I HAVE NOTIFIED THIS BEAUTIFUL PHOTO, WHERE THERE IS A LORD WHO HAS THIS LOVELY HAND IN THEIR HANDS. AND SHE?

The customer may remember a pleasant moment, going into detail. Maybe he will say, YES, I WAS. I HAVE I FISHED IT. The seller will continue to hold the anchor firmly in the memories of the interlocutor with a phrase of the type HOW'O BRAVO. THINK ABOUT THAT SATISFACTION MUST HAVE LIVED. And the customer will return to the place of fishing, deepening the theme with a phrase like "THE SUMMER OF 2014, I AND THREE FRIENDS..."

In short, this anchorage gave the environment a relaxing environment, essential for undertaking a sales negotiation. You will also agree that anchoring has helped to increase the chances of completing the deal. True?

Another example. You are a novice seller and you are going to sell a new car to the customer. What do you need in the sales negotiation? Being novice, almost certainly of tranquility. Try to think of a time when you felt a deep relaxation condition. Maybe when you were on the beach last summer or when you were in the mountains with your friends. Think hard at that moment. Then create an anchor. Such as? Maybe crossing your fingers or holding your fists. Do it several times, so that the anchor, which is certainly not created from scratch, is as stable as possible in your mind. Clench your fists and think about the positive memory, clench your fists and think once again about the pleasant memory, continue to perform the operation twenty times. Then what happens? That keeping your fists closed, the pleasant memory will be even stronger, that you will feel maximum relaxation around you and you will be yourself when you sell the car. The performance anxiety typical of new salespeople can drive you away even in this way.

This anchor is among the most immediate to create. As a logical consequence, it is also de-planned to be extremely easy. The more the anchoring is strange and out of the canonical patterns, the more powerful and difficult to de-program is confirmed. To conclude, the anchors prove to be indispensable tools in Neuro-Linguistic Programming applied to sales in order to re-access to enhanced states that allow the customer to relive pleasant moments and to start with a good footing a business-oriented negotiation. In the role of the seller, it's up to you to decide when to call them into question. Play this joker well and make the most of the potential in your commercial soul.

Hypnotic questions and persuasive sales

One of the most common defects that customers find in many sellers lies in excessive talkativeness. Talking too much is never positive. The most common reason is that this category of sellers suffers from performance anxiety.

To get to the conclusion soon and for fear of not being able to complete the sales negotiation, they talk too much and skip some steps that are fundamental in the negotiation.

These sellers are not updated. They are not in step with the times. The reason? They use démodé sales techniques, which were widely used around the sixties when customers did not have enough information (TV was a niche tool and the internet didn't even exist) and the salesman could afford the luxury of repaying them of beautiful words.

What should be done when selling according to the principles of NLP?

First, ask questions about the context.

The question: DOCTOR ROSSI, WHAT IS YOUR COMPANY WORKING FOR? is always welcome. The reason? Allow the customer to speak freely.

The client entrepreneur could respond in this way: WE ARE SPECIALIST WHOLESALERS IN THE SALE OF SPORTS EQUIPMENT AND FITNESS ARTICLES THAT OPERATE AT LOCAL LEVEL.

At this point, the skilled salesman tries to go deeper into the issue, placing general questions first to better analyze the situation.

A question like WHAT KIND OF SPORTS EQUIPMENT AND FITNESS ARTICLES? could be useful to go deeper and to break the ice.

The answer could be MULTISPORT ELECTRONIC BOARDS, RESERVE BENCHES

AND TRAINERS, STEEL CAGE DOOR CALLS, PALLANUOTO BALLS, SOCCER FIELDS, CORNER FLAGS, REFEREE ITEMS, TENNIS NETS and much more.

The skilled salesman understood the general picture of the situation and deduced that the wholesaler turned to gyms, swimming pools, sports fields. But nevertheless, he asks and checks if his customer base is even more.

For example, DOES YOUR COMPANY ALSO HAVE SHOPS? allows the seller to have a complete picture of the target company he is interfacing with.

The wholesaler's answer could be affirmative: ABSOLUTELY Yes. WE SELL TO MORE THAN 500 STORES IN THE WHOLE TUSCANY.

At this point, the seller puts into practice refined Neuro-Linguistic Programming tools concerning a personal episode that is pleasant.

For example:

WATCH, RIGHT WHEN I WAS IN THE HALL, I NOTICE A SPLENDID BOY PHOTO ON A TRAMPOLINE, LITTLE BEFORE DIVING IN THE WATER. WHAT HAD AN OFFICIAL COMPETITION? (Please note the anchor).

The customer who perhaps cares about this photoshoot will be inclined to respond, perhaps saying: LOOK, IT WAS MY SON, COMMITTED IN AN AGONISTIC COMPETITION...

And the seller, taking the customer to think positively, will seize the chance to say: ACCIDENTS WHAT SATISFACTION!

Then, he will return to his primary intent, asking questions about the problems. So, you could say a sentence like: YOU TOLD ME YOU WILL TAKE OVER 500 STORES IN TUSCANY. WELL, HOW DO YOU DELIVER? The undeclared intent is to bring out the actual needs of the wholesaler.

The latter could answer in this way: THE DELIVERY WE MANAGE IT IN THE FIRST PERSON I AM AND MY MEMBER, FRIEND OF

THE OLD DATE. WE HAVE A HEADED CORPORATE VAN.

The seller goes even deeper, focusing on the timing when the volume of business for the wholesaler is higher. Without being too indiscreet, he asks: CAN I ASK YOU, SO MUCH FOR CURIOSITY, WHAT IS THE PERIOD IN WHICH YOU WORK MORE?

The customer who has trusted the seller will reply: WITHOUT THE SHADOW OF SUMMER THAT SUMMER. TUSCANY IS FULL OF BATHROOMS AND, CONSEQUENTLY, IT WORKS A LOT IN SUMMER. EVEN TOO MUCH. OFTEN, WE ALSO EXPECT TO GO FOR YOU.

With this last sentence, the customer unconsciously reveals one of his weaknesses to the seller that we remember is a complete stranger. This indicates that the seller has been adept at creating an excellent interpersonal communication relationship.

The seller at this point in the negotiation shows in a self-evident way that the wholesaler finds himself faced with a problem rather difficult to face. The question I was right in asking myself how do you do in this period to complete all the deliveries? is the center.

The wholesaler will give his explanation: IN SUMMER THREE PEOPLE GIVE US A HAND. WE ARE SEASONAL WORKERS WHICH WE ASSUME ONLY IN THE MONTHS OF JUNE, JULY, AND AUGUST. EVERYONE HAS A PERSONAL VAN. THEREFORE, IN SUMMER WE ARE IN FIVE THAT DELIVER.

On the same logic as the other questions, another well-posed question, according to the principles of NLP is to put the finger on the question thoroughly. THEN IN THE SUMMER SUCCESS, SEPPUR FOR THE HEADSET BROKEN TO COMPLETE ALL DELIVERIES, RIGHT?

The client can only nod, responding affirmatively even if not very enthusiastic.

What has emerged at this point is that the problem is there and the solution up to this point is not the non plus ultra, SO MUCH IT IS TRUE THAT SOME DELIVERIES WE HAVE HAD TO JUMP IT. THE MOLE OF WORK IN SUMMER WAS TOO MUCH.

Now comes the numerical part. Using the powerful tools of Neuro-Linguistic Programming, the astute salesman will ask the question: WHAT IS IT ACTUALLY LOSES HIS COMPANY IN ECONOMIC TERMS IN THE MOMENT WHEN THE DELIVERY DOES NOT GO TO THE PORT? CAN I GIVE ME ESTIMATED AN ESTIMATE? SO MUCH FOR...

The aim of the aforementioned question is, therefore, to make the client concentrate on the obstacle that his entrepreneurial reality has before him.

The entrepreneur, with a light heart, could respond in this way. AT OCCHIO TEMO, AHIME', THAT A FAILED DELIVERY COSTS NOT LESS THAN 3,000 EUROS. BUT IN SOME CASES, EVEN SOMETHING MORE.

At this point the seller verifies the extent of the actual problem, asking: IS NOT A BIT TOO MANY?

The customer, a little disappointed, will confirm: YES, FOR A SMALL COMPANY LIKE OURS, THE SUSSISTE PROBLEM.

At this point, hypnotic questions come to life. The seller always lets the customer talk. This is, in fact, the basic idea in the field of Neuro-Linguistic Programming. Ask a question about the possible solution to the problem, as I tell you, how could the problem be solved? is a correct way to ask oneself. The reason? The entrepreneur will feel valued by the question, because he knows that the seller is interested in knowing his opinion, as well as focused on his concrete needs.

Ergo, your possible answer could be the aforementioned: ESTIMATE IN THE SUMMER THE NUMBER OF DELIVERIES TO BE MADE IS WHAT YOU HAVE COMPLEX.

ONE PERSON WOULD HAVE NEEDED MORE THAN, BUT NOT FIXED, THAT MAY OCCUR TO WORK ON A CALL. IN THE MOMENTS OF PEAK, WITH A TELEPHONE CALL I WOULD CALL THIS PERSON WHO WITH A PRIVATE VAN YOU MIGHT GIVE ME A BIG HAND. IN THIS WAY, I WILL NOT RECEIVE YOU AT THE FIXED COSTS TO BE ADDRESSED AND MY PROFITS WERE NOT THEREFORE LONGER AFFECTED.

Now comes the highlight of the sales negotiation. The seller is called upon to explain accurately which service he proposes, however prompting Dr. Rossi to request information on the product/service offered. With a phrase of the caliber DOCTOR ROSSI, SORRY WHY NOT HAVE THE SERVICE THAT YOUR BUSINESS NEEDS, the seller gains the attention of the Tuscan wholesaler who can do nothing but ask for a light.

The seller will explain the advantages of his commercial offer: OUR SERVICE CLICK FAST

DELIVERY ALLOWS YOU TO CONTACT AN EXPERT DELIVERED PERSON WHICH, EQUIPPED WITH ITS CALL, ALSO LAST MINUTE, COMPLETES DELIVERY THROUGHOUT THE TUSCANY.

From there on, the wholesaler will ask for information on prices, availability and in all likelihood will contact the delivery operator during the summer.

The seller on duty worked with hypnotic questions. What are? Simple, dry questions that go straight to the heart of the matter and capture the attention of the potential shift client who has the freedom to express himself freely.

This is one of the most correct modus operandi that, in the role of an active professional in the field of commercial sales, you can follow during a negotiation. Make use of a sequence of questions that lead the potential customer to take an interest in the solution to be proposed.

To frame the context in the first place (Who is the customer? In which sector?), To bring the potential customer to have Houston say, we have a problem, to make him say in his voice that something is wrong, to examine the effects that the problem causes (as if to put the finger in the wound), ask the customer what solutions he would have in mind (knowing the product he is ready to present) allows you to rotate around the customer, understanding their real needs.

And are you able to persuade the customer? A lot of betting on hypnotic questions is really worth it if you care about the need to complete the transaction successfully.

The Switch Mode

When you sell, you have to pay attention to automatic behaviors that tend to trigger regardless of your actual awareness. Starting from the assumption that the mind easily learns behaviors, here is a useful example of the topic.

Suppose a man, after a hard day's work, comes home and waits for nothing but going to bed. However, when he goes into the bedroom, he finds her untidy and starts to curse. The sequence is based on the following steps: OPENING OF THE ENTRANCE DOOR -> ENTRY IN THE CORRIDOR -> GREETING TO THE WIFE AND CHILDREN -> ENTRY IN THE BEDROOM -> ABSOLUTE CHAIR VIEW -> INQUIRIES.

If the scene is repeated several times, it will become an uncontrollable automatism. The problem is that the mind also learns destructive behaviors that can seriously jeopardize relationships. Not only in the field of sales between buyer and seller, but also at a professional or family level. In order to avoid damaging oneself and relationships with others, the behavior must be reconverted. In this case, the tired man expects to find order in the house. Having identified the typical sequence of events, already described, the switch mode model in the NLP field assumes that the intervention is not performed on the negative state. The reason for this choice is very simple: it is now too late.

A valid alternative must be planned well before. The alternative must be triggered in this case in the ABSOLUTE CHAIR VIEW step. When the tired man sees the disorder, he will have to associate a pleasant alternative. Putting things in order with your wife and children is one of them. In other words, behaviors that are constructive and non-destructive. The switch model in NLP does nothing but pull the destructive behavior out of the mind of the person concerned (in this case the swearing at the sight of the disorder), keeping it away, and it almost seems to install in his mind a pleasant alternative (in our example, teamwork with the family in tidying up the bedroom). The installation process of the new image, which is associated with a pleasant feeling, must be repeated over and over again: at first at normal speed, then gradually at a more accelerated pace. Then, by putting yourself to the test, you will almost certainly see that you will automatically trigger a new behavior.

Potentiating or de-potentiating state?

Neuro-Linguistic Programming includes two states: the empowering state and the de-potentiating state.
What differences exist? Let's start with the generic definition of mood. What is it? Simply the condition, in physical and mental terms, in which the interlocutor and the client are at a precise moment.
Entering the theme, for the purposes of the principles of NLP, the de-potentiating state is defined as K-, in that it is a dysfunctional psycho-physical condition. A customer does not seem particularly focused on the item you wish to sell or the technical features of the service you are presenting. His gaze seems empty, not even staring at you. With a joke, in the role of the seller, you can change the rapport, bringing it in fact from a de-potentiating state to an empowering

one, known in NLP as K +. An optimal psycho-physical condition of the customer certainly increases the possibility that the negotiation in the sale is successfully completed.

An example of depowering status is the aforementioned: you are working on the PC, but your ADSL line is not the best. The connection always falls. Then it happens that a telephone salesman calls you right when the internet connection is lost and that movie that you were enjoying by streaming is interrupted. You, theoretically, would have all the interest to listen to it, because you want to change telephone operator and internet. However, you don't and maybe you rudely close the phone call with the most classic I have to do. Have you ever experienced the thing yourself?

The moral of the story is that if you sell, before starting the negotiation, it is wise to check that the client's psycho-physical state is K +, that is to say, empowering. This in no way means that the customer you are interacting with must always be smiling and ready to say yes. It just means that there must be no barriers or obstacles of an external nature when you begin the article presentation operations.

But watch out that knowing how to exploit a depleting state (K-) can make you complete the sale. Do you know how many times smartphone sellers have made their customers feel embarrassed, almost brazenly, because they had an ultra-dated device and almost told them BUT YOU DON'T WASH, THEY TO STILL USE THIS PHONE? The same applies to car dealers. Do you have any idea on how many occasions, the sellers have put their finger on the scourge of customers who were driving real knots? We need to know how to do it, though. We must use the right language when it comes to limestone in a de-potentiating state.

An ill-posed observation or misinterpretation by the other party will only affect the positive outcome of commercial negotiation.

Deepening the discourse of the deponent state, there are harmful words in a commercial negotiation.

Here they are in a quick overview:

· NO.

A customer saw a nice pair of jeans in the window. However, in the blue color, he prefers the black one, because maybe more in line with his style. So, enter the store and ask. GOOD MORNING. BEAUTIFUL THOSE JEANS. ARE THEY AVAILABLE IN BLACK COLORING? And the seller replies with a peremptory NO. Result? The customer will say goodbye and leave. NO is a word that must be banned from the seller's vocabulary. In any sales negotiation, there are always tricks that lead to saying yes. Which doesn't mean that when you sell, you're lying, but you need to be cunning not to burn the sale. NO, at the neuro-linguistic level, is a response that has a devastating negative impact on the brain of the listener. A closing mechanism is implemented that takes the customer away. The interlocutor will feel rejected. It's a fact.

When you sell, you always propose constructive alternatives, aimed at enhancing an empowering state (K+). Returning to the question BEAUTIFUL THESE JEANS, ARE THEY AVAILABLE IN BLACK COLORING? Instead of answering NO, a constructive alternative is AT THIS MOMENT, THEY ARE AVAILABLE IN BLUE AND WHITE. The word NO, I didn't even appear. WANT TO TRY THEM? The customer could find the alternative WHITE COLOR rather valid and interesting.

· DISORDER

Think carefully. There is a scenario in which you can consider the disorder as a source of well-being. The answer is obvious: absolutely not. Ergo, don't complicate your life when you sell. Banish this word from your vocabulary.

THE DISORDER TO KNOW IF IT IS INTERESTED IN OUR LAST TELEPHONE INTERNET SUBSCRIPTION SERVICE. The beginning is an own goal. The better the form THE CONTACT TO KNOW IF IT IS INTERESTED IN OUR LAST SUBSCRIPTION TELEPHONE INTERNET SERVICE.

Sounds different, doesn't it?

· SORRY / EXCUSE

If you think about it, when are you apologizing? When you make a mistake when you make a mistake. The impact of the word SCUSA / SCUSI in neurological terms is certainly not positive, because it has the aftertaste of a justification. Even if spoken politely and formally.

Excuse me if I allow myself, BUT IN PLACE OF BLACK JEANS, I HAVE BLACK FLANELLA PANTS. WANT TO TRY THEM?

From your sales process, the word SCUSA / SCUSI must be removed as long as it sounds like you're justifying yourself in the customer's impact. Result? Risks of making your negotiation ineffective. This is not an excess of education. In this case, better to go to the point, saying. LOOK, I HAVE BLACK FLANELLA PANTS. WANT TO TRY THEM?

· IF I WERE YOU / YOU

As a seller, you are being suffocated because you are putting yourself in the customer's shoes. Result? Total disaster. GOOD MORNING. BEAUTIFUL THOSE JEANS. ARE THEY AVAILABLE IN BLACK COLORING? An answer like that IF I WERE IN YOU, OPTEREI FOR THAT BEAUTIFUL PAIR OF BLACK PANTS IN FUSTAGNO is not professional, because it shows that the initial demand of the customer just does not have the slightest interest. You are assuming you know the customer's tastes. It is the customer who must always and, in any case, have the right to choose what he wants and to decide what is most in line with what his tastes or needs are.

Better to say in our example NOW WE SEE IF THIS LOVELY PAIR OF BLACK TROUSERS IN MUSHROOM IS OWN AT ITS CASE.

· I EXPLAIN TO YOU

This formula also creates a state of anger in the customer, because the latter will assume that the seller considers him as someone who cannot understand. Or at most, that you as a salesman know everything and that he, as a customer really little or nothing.

I EXPLAIN TO YOU. YESTERDAY, A CUSTOMER HAS PURCHASED THE LAST PAIR OF BLACK JEANS. Better to say LOOK, I ORDERED THEM YESTERDAY, GIVEN THAT A CUSTOMER WAS AWARDED THE LAST PAIR.

Another shining example. At the entry formula LOOK, I EXPLAIN THE HARDWARE FEATURES OF THIS SPLENDID TABLET. Better to replace the softer form LOOK, I EXPECT BETTER ABOUT THE HARDWARE FEATURES OF THIS SPLENDID TABLET.

Returning to the VAK's discourse, in this case, if the client is visual, say THE MONSTERS THE HARDWARE CHARACTERISTICS OF THIS SPLENDID TABLET, if it is audible NOW I LIST ONE TO YOU THE HARDWARE CHARACTERISTICS OF THIS TABLET, DEEPENING THEM IN DETAILS, if it is kinesthetic TEST WITH HAND THAT CHARACTERISTICS HARDWARE HAS THIS TABLET, gives you an extra gear in the negotiations. The reason? Take the customer with absolute ease.

· I TELL YOU THE TRUTH

Another unforgivable mistake. This phrase rejects the sale because the customer almost unconsciously assumes that as a rule when you sell, you are a liar. BEAUTIFUL THESE JEANS, ARE THEY AVAILABLE IN BLACK COLORING? Answer LOOK, I TELL YOU THE TRUTH. HAS BOUGHT A CUSTOMER YESTERDAY. The utmost TI I SAY THE TRUTH has the power to nullify everything you said earlier.

How to insert them FRENCH and SINCERELY is better to remove them. Eliminate the superfluous from your vocabulary and communicate by going to the point. As if to point directly to the heart of the matter.

· ANYTHING

Used as interlayer it is synonymous with own goal in the sale.

EH, NOTHING. A CATALOG I HAVE A LOT OF BEAUTIFUL NEWS. WE WANT TO WATCH THEM TOGETHER? Better the form without the negative interlayer A CATALOG I HAVE A LOT OF GOOD NEWS. WE WANT TO WATCH THEM TOGETHER?

In conclusion, if you sell, remember not to use these harmful words. NEVER. The impact on the customer is disastrous. The first words you communicate have a very strong impact on the recipient's brain. Then it becomes complex, to go and remove them from his mind. So, in mediation don't start on the wrong foot.

The Rule of Contrast

In the field of Neuro-Linguistic Programming applied to sales, the principle of contrast presupposes that when a seller presents two products in succession, if the second stimulus differs from the first, it follows that it will be seen even more distantly from what it actually is. In essence, putting a sequence of things in a row helps to alter the individual situation. The customer's perception is modified. This is a fact.

In selling, one thing will be to present the customer with only one product at a time. Another thing is to present two products together. Finally, it is very different to present multiple products simultaneously. The customer's perception can only be totally different.

Example

A software company offers a program available in three versions. An entry-level that costs very little, but with minimal features. The other, with a slightly higher price, but still accessible to all, characterized by an important number of functions, excellent for the average user. Finally, the top-of-the-range alternative with a high price, but with features for high-professional users. With these strategies, many companies in the information technology sector can better intercept a much wider catchment area. However, in your opinion, almost always, which version sells more at the software level? Of course, the second one. That average. And not just because the average user in the IT field is part of a larger target. The reason is that almost everyone who surfs the internet will evaluate the benefits and quality of the service offered and then decide. All in all, however, placing the average version of the application at the center between the entry-level and the top of the range is certainly a rewarding strategy.

Skimming and sequencing are one of the pillars of the rule of contrast in NLP. If the customer enters a luxury fashion boutique, where there is a myriad of clothes, presented without logical rigor, after seeing them all in rapid succession, the customer may not buy anything. This is because upstream, the job of skimming, in the role of the seller, you did not own. You have loaded the potential buyer with expectations, but you have not been able to hit his attention in the right ways.

Close the sale

We have seen how closing a sales deal is not always easy. Putting the customer against the wall, opting for a strategy àut àut presents an endless series of risks that can seriously jeopardize the progress of the negotiation and, in the worst case, the crossroads can send the sales negotiation to the air. Ergo, if you are a seller, forget this strategy to avoid your client turning their back on you and turning elsewhere. Of magic words that quickly allow you to close the mediation, unfortunately, there are none. However, some formulas and techniques are decidedly useful to the case that, among other things, allow you to keep performance anxiety away. How many sellers who when they interact with the customer do not see the gold of sighing the fateful phrase ECCO, CE I did it?

The client cannot pass from a demotivated state to an enthusiastic one in no time at all. You will not sign any contract and you will not sell anything to him unless you see him as a person (NB: a person, not a seller) credible. The ideal condition for you seller, namely the customer who buys from you on the fly without asking too many questions (in short, without giving you too much hassle) is a situation that occurs only once. An astral combination that goes through once in a million. Today the customer has internet and is already informed of his. However, it raises questions to learn more and to orientate oneself concerning the competition (which is usually always a lot). Ergo, when you sell a product, you must be prepared. You need to know all its features from a technical point of view. You need to know what's so special that it's unique to competitors. You must identify the focal points for which it is worth buying and transmit them with enthusiasm to your interlocutor. If you don't have this art (because of art it is) ...well, then the world of sales is not what is right for you.

Many sellers, therefore, commit the error of wanting to immediately think about the conclusion of the negotiation, forgetting all the work to be done upstream in view of the conviction and persuasion of the buyer. Poorly managed approaches, such as a delay in an appointment with your client, a clothing that is not entirely online at the moment, a modus operandi that is too urgent and suffocating (especially with the tall customers of the company), a wrong phrase, an erroneous communication are all problems that must never exist, for the simple reason that they already make you leave on the wrong foot. Result? The customer will never buy from you.

It is not hyperbole to believe that the sales negotiation is a process comparable to the construction of a house of cards. There are phases based on logics of balance and joints: if the castle's plans are solid starting from the base, getting to the top will be possible. Likewise, if the initial phase allows you to lower the customer's distrust, the chances of your contract will be decidedly higher. The visual approach and the first contact are decisive steps in the initial phase. And, we have seen how Neuro-Linguistic Programming techniques can give a big hand so that the seller and the customer travel on the same wavelength.

If you don't manage the approach with the customer well, starting from the first few bars, how can you hope that he has the least interest in what you propose to him in commercial terms? How can you hardly believe that you are successful in this context, if first of all you do not intercept its concrete needs, dwelling only on your agenda, your priorities and the characteristics of the product? Upstream, in the sales negotiations, the work of identifying the real needs of the buyers is a condition sine qua non to work well in the field and to present effectively useful proposals, consistent with its values and beliefs, and consequently credible.

Therefore, the visual approach and the first contact, whether you want it or not, are already decisive for the outcome of the negotiation. There you must not go wrong, because the risks of catching a two of spades then become high or at most, if you are optimistic, you will have to worry about completing a recovery that would then be resounding.

The asking of the right questions, letting the client speak freely by using what Socrates defined as the art of maieutic, the framework for identifying the context, the problems, the effects, and solutions, which we have already described in the negotiation between the seller of sports items and equipment to Dr. Rossi, the Tuscan wholesaler, will give you a big hand in reaching the goal. Selling is an art, where first of all it is necessary to create a relaxing atmosphere. Be jovial. Always.

Finally, the closure must be done well to avoid disappointment. But this turns out to be effective only if you worked well upstream. We can compare this operation to a push to a friend who just doesn't feel like jumping into the water. How many times, when you were at sea, did you find yourself in a position to see friends rather reticent, before diving into the water, because maybe they considered it too cold at that time? Well ... give them a boost, it lets you get past this impasse. The moment of hesitation, which willingly or unwillingly registers in all sales negotiations, must be overcome with the most complete nonchalance. All right, you convinced the client, but you don't see the signature on the contract yet. The purchase has not yet completed. And you, then give it a good push! Just like the hesitant friend, a few moments before diving, once he is in the water, he will thank you. Here, the customer will do more or less like this, so to speak.

There is a multitude of closing techniques in the sale. Every seller has his style. We limit ourselves to mentioning an example that can prove particularly tantalizing to your eyes: the so-called Benjamin Franklin closing technique. All-round politician, self-made man, journalist, printer, activist, self-taught scientist and far-sighted inventor for the inventions of the lightning rod, the glasses harmonica, the bifocal lenses, the stove-fireplace (known as Franklin stove) and for the improvement of the odometer, the proposition of summertime, as well as among the Founding Fathers of the United States of America who actively participated in the American Revolution, lived in the eighteenth century, Benjamin Franklin was particularly appreciated for how he conducted the negotiations with the interlocutors. The entire negotiation took place in complete transparency, given that he used to present the points in favor and those against a decision. In this way, he was judged positively, because, as indicated, everyone saw him for what he actually was. An honest man, first of all. Try to conduct a negotiation with the client following the scheme of the sports equipment seller and when you are about to close the negotiation, armed with a pen and paper and put down the advantages of the business proposal under the "+" sign and the disadvantages under the sign " - "(clearly the former must be superior and of higher quality than the latter). Then look your interlocutor in the eye. Let's bet you look at yourself in a different light? The reason? You have distinguished yourself from other sellers, operating uniquely, but at the same time transparent and authoritative. Demonstrating interest in what the customer believes, perhaps by having him write other advantages and disadvantages of the product or service you are offering him, will certainly be a very welcome strategy. There must be few tangible motivations that should lead the interlocutor to give you a refusal. If under the sign "+", of reasons for the purchase there will be many and the customer will think OK, YOU'VE CONVINCED. BUY FROM YOU, IT IS REALLY THE PENALTY, you will have hit the mark!

Please note: this way of conducting the negotiation, known as the Benjamin Franklin method, only comes to fruition if the customer has already gained interest in what you say. You only have to give him the final push and then you will have bingo. Starting on the spot with this technique is pure suicide in terms of negotiation. It is like jumping out of a plane without first checking if the parachute is in trouble. It is like showing romance to a girl, without you having noticed hints of interest in her. For this technique, you must have already

created a beautiful empty highway, to drive towards the finish line. And you can do this with a well-structured job upstream ... even using sales-oriented NLP techniques!
There are also very useful magic words to conclude a sales negotiation.
What are they?

· YES'
All of us, but everyone, in the customer's shoes, we always want to hear each other say yes. Regarding the customer who asked for black jeans, after seeing the blue ones in the window, to the direct question ARE THE BLACK SELLER ALSO AVAILABLE IN THE COLOR?, the experienced seller, despite not having them, can say YES. I ARRIVE TOMORROW, AS YESTERDAY I ORDERED THEM.
At the neurological level, an affirmative answer involves the dilation of the pupils and the relaxation of the facial muscles by the recipient. Finally, a particularly relaxing

environment is created. The predisposition to cash in is the anteroom to reach very important goals when referring to the world of sales.

· Positive adjectives create a predisposition to purchase

- This software is really full of options
- This tablet is fantastic
- Driving this car is a unique experience
- This notebook is the best in its range
- The turtleneck sweater in cashmere is the most elegant seen this year

· Own Name

How many times do you end up getting angry, because that new person has already forgotten your name? It's not that he does it on purpose. It's just that you don't like it, because it's like you're snubbing yourself, not remembering at all who you are?

If you have just met the customer, giving him a name and calling him by name is an approach that many like.

WATCH FRANCESCO, THIS TABLET COMPARED TO LAST YEARS MODEL HAS BETTER PERFORMING GRAPHICS, A MORE POWERFUL PROCESSOR, THE INTERNAL MEMORY IS MORE CAPABLE, AND IT TAKES PHOTOS EVEN BETTER.

· The tracing rules

We have largely disregarded it in our book. However, another classic example: as a seller, a customer calls you CIAO ALESSANDRO I HAVE A PROBLEM WITH THE ADSL LINE. SO, CAN YOU PLEASE GIVE ME A HAND?

The seller will do tracing by saying. HELLO LUIGI. WITH THAT PROBLEM WE WILL FIND THE SOLUTION ON TO FLY!

Conclusions

Summing up, the tools of NLP prove to be indispensable for sellers who wish to successfully complete business, regardless of the sector in which they operate, be it the world of real estate, insurance, professional courses, video games, of food supplements, household products, appliances and telling you.

If you are a beginner in the field of sales or if you are currently working in this field, but you have a somewhat introverted character or if you are shy, the principles of Neuro-Linguistic Programming described in this book can help you have more confidence in your personal and, consequently, to make you relate more directly and...why not, more brazenly with your customers. The common denominator of a successful negotiation in the field of sales is to recognize the customer who is in front of you and know how to treat it differently, even using the techniques learned in this book. The powerful tools of Neuro-Linguistic Programming could be the key to determining excellent results and improving your commercial performance.

Disclaimer

All registered trademarks and logos mentioned in this book, including Amazon, belong to their respective owners.

The author of this book does not claim or declare any rights to these trademarks, which are mentioned only for educational purposes.

www.ingramcontent.com/pod-product-compliance
Lightning Source LLC
Chambersburg PA
CBHW060853220526
45466CB00003B/1350